Praise for *The Rel*

*"What a gem.
Life is all about relationships, and
Justin M.G. Mendez has captured the essence of
getting and keeping the relationships you hunger
for in your life.*

A must read for enriching your life."

Bob Vanourek,
*Award-winning Author of
"Triple Crown Leadership" and Five-time CEO*

*"My husband and my 11 year anniversary is
coming up soon... being reminded about the
small, simple, yet crucial things will truly help
us...*

The book could not have come at a better time."

Laura Michels,
*Kindergarten/Preschool Teacher,
With Husband 11 Years*

"If you improve the quality of your relationships you will improve the quality of your life.

In his book, The Relationship You Really Want, Justin M.G. Mendez shows us the way."

***Michael Alexander**,*
Top Sales Trainer,
Eric Lofholm International

The Relationship You *Really* Want

The Relationship You *Really* Want

5 Simple Steps and 30 Days to More Fulfilling Relationships

Justin M.G. Mendez
Foreword by Tashina E. Combs

First and foremost, thank you
for purchasing this book;
I sincerely appreciate your interest in my work
and admire your willingness to learn and
grow as a person.

This book is not long. You could likely read it in
less than an hour. However I would encourage
you to read it over the course of several weeks. I
would also encourage you to read it the same way
Dale Carnegie encouraged his audience to read
his book, *How to Win Friends and Influence
People*, by first reading each section all the way
through then going back and re-reading it to fully
absorb the section before moving forward.

The format of this book is such that each idea
builds off of the last in one way or another.
Additionally, as you read and are introduced to
new ideas your mind will become more fertile for
the seeds of the next idea. By taking a break to
work on one section you are allowing your mind
to prepare itself for the next. Read a section, put
into action what it has to offer, then move on to
the next section.

ACKNOWLEDGMENTS

I would like to acknowledge the following
individuals, in no particular order.

Each and every one of you has touched my life in
a very special way, for that I am humbly grateful.

Alan Lakien
Anthony Robbins
Bob Vanourek
Cam Altamura
Charles Dickens
Chris Widender
Curt and Natalie Sobolewski
Dale Carnegie
Darren Hardy
Deepak Chopra
Devin Ruiz
Don Miguel Ruiz
Dr. Wayne Dyer
Eddie Keator
Gabrielle Bernstein
Garrett Sutton
Henry Eakland
Jack Canfield
James Malinchak
James Redfield

Jennifer Combs
Jim Rohn
Ken Blanchard
Ken Keyes, Jr.
Les Brown
Michael "Mike Dimas" Harrison
Michael Alexander
My Grandmother and Grandfather
Nic Altamura
Og Mandino
Ovidilio Vasquez
Pema Chödrön
Randie Ellington
Richard Bach
Rick, Debra, Ricky, Kanako, Michael, Jackie,
Layla, and Kara Mendez
Spencer and Kirsten Crowl
Spencer Johnson
Stuart Wilde
Tashina Combs
Taylor Radig
The Free Book Exchange in El Cerrito, CA
Tyree Johnson
Viktor E. Frankl
Zig Ziglar

And everyone else who continues to inspire me,
You know who you are.

CONTENTS

FOREWORD

When Justin asked me to write the foreword for this book, I was surprised. I am not an expert on relationships. I do not have any training in this subject. Nor do I have a background in writing personal development literature.

Justin, on the other hand, is an award-winning speaker with a focus on the principles of personal development and leadership communication. I am many things – a published author, someone who spends far too much time diving into social media each day, a fitness buff, an individual who is constantly trying to learn and grow… I am also Justin's partner of several years. While I may not be an expert on personal development principles or leadership communication, I can give my input on the results of the steps Justin has illustrated in this book and how they changed our relationship for the better.

They say that there is no greater expert than one who has lived the experience for themselves. Justin and I have lived through these steps together as they were formed, went into effect, and as the changes started to compound in our relationship.

If you were to go back two years and place a video of our average night together side-by-side with one of today, you would not even believe that it was the same couple or the same relationship. The steps in this book have greatly improved the quality of our communication and interactions, our level of trust, the way we support one another, and our appreciation for one another.

The idea that the steps in this book, which made such an impact on our relationship, have the chance to positively change so many other relationships out there is truly amazing.

I find it important to remember that it is often the little things that matter most. The little things that may not seem like much at the time add up and have a much greater effect than you ever thought they could. These steps are so simple and offer such great rewards that you owe it to yourself to try them and see the changes with your own eyes and feel them with your own heart.

Tashina E. Combs
World's Leading Authority on Cruelty-Free,
Vegan Beauty and Lifestyle
Creator of Logical Harmony

The Relationship You *Really* Want

Justin M.G. Mendez

INTRODUCTION

I would like to begin by saying five things.

1. I did not wake up one day with this text in my head. Every single idea in this book has been inspired by someone else. Although, in most cases I have built on them and interpreted them through my own system of perception, as you will with this book. I tell you this because the first steps in my own transformation began from reading books others had written and listening to speeches others had delivered. That is a fact I would like to be well known. If you want to change your life, begin by reading books and listening to speeches.

2. As I am a man, this book is written from a male perspective with a male narrative. I sincerely believe that every gender will benefit from the following pages and have done everything I can to appeal to everyone.

3. I made the steps in this book as simple as I could possibly think of. I know you're busy. I know you have a job and a social life and probably too few hours in the day. I also know that this book will only be useful if you actually take action. It is not enough to simply know something. It does not matter if you "know how to communicate" unless you actually use those skills. You have already taken the first step by beginning to read this book, so go ahead, continue on your journey and resolve to take action- your future self will thank you.

4. This is not a *30 days and you're done* book, and I will not give you a new challenge every single day. This book is a guide to building new habits over the course of 30 days which you will continue to consistently practice in order to transform your relationship *and* maintain it.

5. This book is dedicated to Tashina Combs. Tashina is the editor of this book and the author of the forward. She and I became romantically involved about three years prior to the writing of this book. Which means she and I were together before I started my own transformation and before she began hers. Without Tashina's love, support, and patience my life would not be nearly as wonderful as it is today. Tashina, I love you.

PREFACE

I have had many failed relationships. Many of my close friends do not know this, but I have actually had two failed engagements.

So what would possess me to write a book titled *The Relationship You Really Want*?

Who am I to make suggestions about how to have a fulfilling relationship?

I am simply a man who decided to take responsibility for his life and change the only thing within his power to change: *Himself*. Through this process of self-transformation I realized that it was a simple choice to have better relationships.

I also realized that if I could change, I could help others change as well. That is the purpose of this book.

A few years ago I would have been the last person anyone would have asked for relationship advice, especially those who knew me best.

And yet today I have the kind of relationship most people dream of. My relationship is full of love and support, and held together by trust and respect.

The strange thing is that while the transformation of my relationships has been incredible, it is not the result of any huge acts. I did not decide to spend an hour every single day talking with my partner, I did not plan extravagant vacations for us, and we did not agree to have sex seven days a week.

At certain points in any relationship I think it is important to do each of the above mentioned activities; yes, even having sex seven days a week. We all need to interrupt our pattern from time to time. But none of the aforementioned is what transformed my relationship, and I doubt they would transform yours for any extended period of time.

It was the small steps that lead to the transformation. It was each tiny act, done on a consistent basis, that slowly but surely turned distrust to trust, miscommunication to clear understanding, and grudges into forgiveness. Sharing with you those small steps is the focus of this book.

Use the contents of this book and I promise you, you will see and experience positive change in your relationships.

Justin M.G. Mendez
Justin Mendez, LLC

One

Preparation

Today is more a day of preparation, reflection and getting things in order than anything else. The first thing I want you to think about is this: Are you ready to take 100% responsibility for the way you feel and the condition of your relationship? If your answer is no, put this book down and pick it back up when the answer has changed to yes or when you are at least open to the idea.

The next step in your preparation is also a matter of mindset. Get prepared to ask yourself every day for the next thirty days, "What is one thing I can do today to make my partner's life easier?" and "What is one thing I can do today that would give my partner a reason to feel special?" Keep in mind these do not need to be huge acts, in fact it's better that they aren't. If you try to go too big in the beginning it is going to be a lot harder to keep the pace. Think of the next thirty days as a marathon, not a sprint. Start with small steps like taking out the trash when it's your partner's turn or writing a note of appreciation and leaving it somewhere your partner will find it throughout the day.

I know you are probably anxious to actually take a step forward so here's today's opportunity:

Grab your planner and find a day on which you know you can spare five minutes. This is going to be the day you send a postcard to your partner's office. My day is Thursday. I picked Thursday because it means that my postcard will arrive at my partner's office at the beginning of the following week. Now go online (I prefer Amazon.com) and buy a pack of at least four postcards. My guess is that you and your partner are going to love this so much you are going to want to keep doing it, so go ahead and buy a few extras.

Also, as if this could not get any easier, you can also buy postage on the USPS website (at the time of this book being published postcards cost thirty-three cents to mail within the US). By the way, if you don't know your partner's work address look it up online or message one of their colleagues on LinkedIn and swear them to secrecy.

BONUS! Here's a great tip I first heard about from Darren Hardy's book, The Compound Effect. Go out and get a journal, and for the next 30 days write one thing you love about your partner. Keep this journal as secret as possible and gift it to your partner at the end of the 30 days. Two things will happen- you will find that you are constantly on the lookout for the good things your partner does and you will have a wonderfully thoughtful gift for them at the end of the 30 days.

At the end of Section One:
You have now committed to taking 100% responsibility for the way you feel and the condition of your relationships.

You are ready to do one thing to make your partner's life easier and one thing to give them a reason to feel special each day for the next thirty days.

You've ordered some postcards and postage stamps online. Or you've gone and purchased them at a brick and mortar location.

You have selected one day in your week on which to schedule five minutes to write a postcard to your partner.

If you are not sure what to write, here are some examples:

- I am really proud of you for…
- I had a great time last weekend when we…
- In the near future let's…
- I love and appreciate you because…

A Note on Taking 100% Responsibility

It has been said that the change from childhood to adulthood is marked by one's decision to take 100% responsibility for their life. But this can be a difficult decision to make, especially if you feel like life has dealt you an unusually difficult hand.

It may feel like taking 100% responsibility for your life means taking the blame for whatever has happened to you. That is not what I am saying. What I am saying is that regardless of what has happened to you and regardless of what others have done, you can still choose how your life will turn out.

My Mother is a perfect example of this. She and her twin brother were put up for adoption when they were two and a half years old. They were put into a foster home with two alcoholic foster parents who were verbally, emotionally, and physically abusive.

For years they endured this abuse. When they were in their teens her brother decided to take his own life by overdosing and shooting himself. You see, he had epilepsy, but his foster parents said he was just having seizures for attention. My Mother was now alone in the foster home.

Finally when she was 18 she decided to find her biological parents. She knew that when she found them she would see that they were wonderful, loving people.

But after tracking them down she discovered that her biological mother was mentally unfit to have children and that her biological father never wanted them. She and her brother were only two of the four children the couple had given birth to. All four had been given up for adoption.

You could say that my Mother was dealt an unfair hand by life. After all she had been through no one would be surprised if she had become an abusive alcoholic just like the people who raised her. But my Mother decided to take responsibility for her life and as a result she is in an incredibly kind, patient, sober, understanding woman.

She is an inspiration to me every day because she took the hand she was dealt and realized that it was up to her to make her dreams come true. In her case those dreams consisted of being a Mother, and being part of a loving family. In spite of her past, she took responsibility for her future. Each of us has the power to do the same.

Taking 100% responsibility can be difficult for many of us because we are not happy with our current circumstances, like the state of our relationship, and we feel that the other person is to blame. Many people think things like, "Well if she would just change then our relationship would be perfect." I was one of those people myself! I used to say things to myself like, "I would give her the attention she wants if she would just stop being so clingy."

Anytime we say these "I would… if they would…" statements we are allowing the actions of others to dictate our feelings and actions. In essence, we are giving up our power to *choose* how we feel and act; we are making other people responsible for our feelings and our actions.

It seems so easy to place responsibility for our problems on other people. It is so easy to say, "I am not the problem, you are." But this is only going to get you so far. If you want your relationship to change, you must be willing to change yourself. That is what taking 100% responsibility is all about.

I have talked a lot about why taking 100% responsibility can be difficult. But the truth is that it is a lot easier to take responsibility for our own life than it is to put the blame on others. The reason for this is that we cannot control what other people do. We cannot even control how they feel. We can give them reasons to feel a certain way or to do certain things but how they respond to those reasons is entirely up to them. For example, if I tell my partner she is beautiful I am giving her a reason to feel beautiful, loved, and appreciated. But it is still her choice to feel those things. If we blame the actions of others for our problems then they must change in order for the problem to be resolved. And since we cannot control what other people do and we cannot make them change, we have effectively given up any chance of a resolution.

On the other hand, when we take responsibility for ourselves we are taking away the power that others have over our lives. We are saying, "No matter what others do or say, I am the only person who can choose my feelings, my actions, and my future." It is an incredibly liberating feeling and you'll start to see your life turn around for the better.

Section One Tweetable: "I am ready to take 100% responsibility for the state of my relationships and my life. I choose to be the solution. **@JustinMGMendez"**

Journal

_____

_____

_____

_____

_____

_____

_____

_____

_____

_____

_____

_____

_____

_____

_____

_____

_____

_____

_____

_____

_____

_____

_____

_____

_____

_____

_____

_____

_____

_____

Regardless of what has happened to you and regardless of what others have done, you can still choose how your life will turn out.

_____

_____

_____

_____

_____

_____

_____

_____

_____

_____

_____

*Are you ready to take 100%
responsibility for the way you feel
and
the condition of your relationship?*

_____

_____

_____

_____

_____

_____

_____

Two

Building and Rebuilding Trust

Healthy relationships have trust. **So, this section is about building trust.** The great thing about trust is that it can be built over time through a series of small, simple steps. If trust has been lost in your relationship you must understand that the process of rebuilding trust is going to take more work and more time. Stick with it and like everything else in this book, it will pay off.

This book is a reflection of my personal experiences. Although I will not go into any great detail, suffice to say that I lost the trust of my partner after making one poor choice to be dishonest and have had to slowly but surely rebuild the trust we once had. I tell you this because I really want you to understand that losing trust does not *necessarily* mean losing a relationship.

If you are committed to your relationship and are willing to put in the time and effort, you can rebuild trust.

I also want to make it clear that in order to rebuild trust your partner must be willing to forgive you. And I mean *sincerely willing* to forgive you. No matter what you do to rebuild trust, if your partner cannot forgive you, or if you cannot forgive yourself, for whatever took place to cause the loss of trust in the first place, you will not be able to move forward in the relationship. This is obviously my opinion, but that's why you got this book, right?

Sometimes trust is lost and it is just not going to be rebuilt because one or both people are unwilling to do what it takes to rebuild it. If you realize that your relationship is in this state you need to make the choice and ask yourself: Is it better to stay in a relationship with no trust or is it better to move on?

As stated above, trust can be developed and cultivated via small steps and the process can be summed up simply: Stay true to your word; do what you say you are going to do when you say you are going to do it and be consistent. Are there other ways to build trust? Of course. But this is the one that worked for me in my relationship.

Think about this example, do you have a friend who is always late? Most people do. When that friend says they'll be at a restaurant at 11:30 do you believe them? Probably not. Why not? Because they have consistently said one thing and done another. We no longer give value (in this case, trust) to what they say they will do in this situation. Your friend can begin to regain your trust by consistently arriving when they say they will arrive.

As with this example, you can start to build more trust in your relationship by making commitments and sticking to them on a regular basis. I realize that this concept sounds overly simple, but I am of the mindset that many things in life are not as complicated as people make them out to be. So while this concept is simple, it also works. Doing what you say you will do when you say you will do it on a consistent basis builds trust.

At the end of Section Two:
You recognize that healthy relationships thrive on trust and that trust can be built through small actions practiced on a daily basis.

You have resolved to start building more trust in your relationship by making small (and perhaps larger) commitments to your partner, and by following through with such commitments consistently. Start this process by making and keeping at least two commitments to your partner per week.

Section Two Tweetable: "Trust is key to healthy relationships. I build trust every day through small, consistent acts. I am trustworthy. **@JustinMGMendez**"

Journal

_____

_____

_____

_____

_____

_____

_____

_____

_____

_____

_____

_____

_____

_____

_____

_____

Stay true to your word; do what you say you are going to do when you say you are going to do it and be consistent.

_____

_____

_____

_____

_____

_____

_____

_____

_____

_____

_____

_____

_____

_____

_____

_____

_____

_____

_____

_____

_____

Three

Communication

I'm sure you've heard the phrase, "It's not *what* you say; it's *how* you say it." Being aware of how we communicate is crucial, but today we are going to focus on the *what*. More specifically, today is about taking words *out* of your vocabulary when using them in a negative context. The two words I encourage you to eliminate are "always" and "never". As in, "You *always* leave dirty dishes out," or "You *never* spend time with me".

These types of statements are very condemning. And when we make condemning statements like these we are, at least for that moment, ignoring the good things our partner does and looking at the relationship from a very black and white perspective.

Additionally, condemning statements communicate a negative expectation. It is as if we are telling our partner, "This is what I expect of you. This is the kind of person you are." People tend to meet the expectations we set for them, so you want to be intentional in the expectations you set and you want to be sure those expectations are positive.

By the way, go ahead and continue using "always" and "never" for phrases like, "You're always so supportive," or "You never disappoint me".

At the end of Section Three:
You have decided to only use words like "always" and "never" in a positive context and to be intentional in the expectations you set for others and yourself.

Let your partner and your friends know that this is something you are working on. Ask them to give you a gentle reminder when you slip. Ask that they use good judgment in regards to *when* they give this gentle reminder.

Follow the link for a free 2 minute video version of this section: http://youtu.be/4wyI7uk7TdM

Section Three Tweetable: "I use intentional communication to set positive expectations for friends, family, colleagues. **@JustinMGMendez**"

Journal

_____

_____

_____

_____

_____

_____

_____

_____

_____

_____

_____

_____

_____

_____

_____

_____

_____

_____

_____

_____

_____

_____

_____

_____

_____

_____

_____

_____

*People tend to meet the expectations
we set for them…
Be intentional in the expectations
you set and be sure they are positive.*

_____

_____

_____

_____

_____

_____

_____

_____

_____

_____

_____

_____

_____

_____

_____

_____

_____

_____

_____

_____

Four

You Will Find What You Are Looking For

Have you ever noticed that negative people seem to find more reasons to be negative while positive people seem to find more reasons to be positive? Why is that?

The answer is that we tend to find what we're looking for. It's like when you decide to buy a particular red car and suddenly you start to see that very same red car everywhere you go. Did these cars magically appear? Of course not; you are just more open to seeing them.

Our beliefs about people, relationships, and the world in general work the same way. If you are more open to seeing your partner as trustworthy you will look for reasons to trust them. If you are more open to seeing them as untrustworthy you will look for reasons to support that belief as well.

Let me give you an example from my own life.

One day I decided I wanted to surprise my partner by getting her a gift. I decided to go to one of her favorite stores and buy one of her favorite bath bombs. When I got to the store the saleswoman showed me their special line of limited edition bath bombs for the upcoming holiday season. I decided to get two bath bombs, one that I would give my partner right away and another that I would hide for a few weeks and give to her as a special holiday gift.

When I got home I presented the first bath bomb to my partner which she accepted with a smile and a kiss. Mission accomplished.

Later that evening as my partner and I were lying in bed she rolled over and asked if I had bought a bath bomb for myself as well the one I had bought for her.

I said no, which was the truth.

To which she replied, "Well you bought two, didn't you?"

Again, I responded with a "No". I did not want to give away the surprise.

She asked again, "But you bought two bath bombs, right?"

"No I didn't."

"Yes you did."

"No. I did not."

"Hunnie," She said, with a slightly disappointed tone, "You left the receipt on the counter. I know you bought two bath bombs."

Let's pause the conversation right there for a moment. What do you suppose my partner was thinking at this point?

From her point of view I had gone out to an expensive store, bought two relatively personal gifts, presented her with one, and then lied repeatedly about having purchased the other. Something was obviously going on here.

"Alright," I said, "You caught me. I bought two bath bombs for you, but one is special so I was saving it to give to you in a few weeks. I can't believe I left that receipt on the counter!"

"Oh," She replied, "I thought maybe you had just bought one for your Mom. Or that you had bought two and forgot the other one at the store and were too embarrassed to admit it to me."

The moral of this story is that my partner sees me as a trustworthy person. And as such, she looks for reasons to trust me. So when situations like this happen, her mind goes to scenarios in which trust would be maintained. She could have handled the situation very differently. She could have grown very upset with me. After all, I had just been caught in a lie. But instead she thought up something as silly as me forgetting a bath bomb at the store and being too proud to admit it. What does that say about what she was looking for in our relationship? And how could this situation have played out differently if she had been looking for something else?

Side note: If I am not too proud to walk into a store and pay $7 for something to make my bath water pink and sparkly, I am definitely not too proud to admit that I forget one at the store!

We all have a choice of what to look for in our relationships, and in life as a whole. My suggestion is that if you must make assumptions about the meaning and motives behind another person's actions, always assume the best.

By choosing to stay positive and give people the benefit of the doubt you open your mind to seeing the best in people. And, of course, we tend to find what we are looking for.

At the end of Section Four:

You understand that people find what they are looking for and as a result have resolved to look for the best in people.

Take something you would like to have in your relationship or something you would like to see in your partner and start looking for it.

You can begin this process by asking yourself questions at the end of each day. For example, let's say you want to feel loved. At the end of every day ask yourself, "What are three things my partner did today to show me that I am loved?" Then answer the question. Throughout the following days you will find that you are looking for reasons to feel loved, and you are likely to find them!

If you want to feel more trust, start looking for trust. Ask yourself at the end of every day, "What are three things my partner did today to show that they are trustworthy?"
The key here is to actually answer these questions. Don't give up if your first response is, "Nothing." Just push a little harder and find the good in your relationship.

Write down what you come up with in the Journal section of this chapter.

Section Four Tweetable: "I know that I will find what I look for. I choose to focus on the positive aspects of life and look for the good in others. **@JustinMGMendez**"

Journal

_____

_____

_____

_____

_____

_____

_____

_____

_____

_____

_____

_____

_____

_____

_____

_____

_____

_____

_____

_____

_____

_____

_____

_____

Ask yourself,
"What are three things my partner
did today to show me that I am
loved?"

_____

_____

_____

_____

_____

_____

_____

_____

_____

Five

Communication and Mindset

The way we see the world is different at different times and is based around what we are focused on at that point.

For example, imagine one day on your way to work someone decides to make an unsafe lane change forcing your car onto the shoulder of the road and almost into a guardrail, on another day a different driver in front of you pays your bridge toll.

Obviously these are two totally different people and you can hold two completely different opinions of them in your head, but each experience will play a role in your view of other drivers in general, strangers, and society as a whole.

What conclusion will you come to? Will you decide that other drivers are rude and selfish, or will you decide that drivers are courteous and kind? Of course you can also decide to believe that the world is full of different people; some of which are rude and some of which are kind, and that's okay. But most people do not take this third option.

Most people believe one or the other. And in order to choose one perspective we must ignore the evidence of the opposing perspective or at least give it only a slight acknowledgment. In other words, our opinions and judgments of people are not based on their actions, but rather on which of their actions we choose to focus.

Today is all about *subtly* shifting the focus from the negative to the positive. I say *subtly* because this will have a very subtle impact on your relationship, but the real purpose of it is to get your mind in the habit of focusing on the positive aspects of life and on the things you do want, instead of the things you do not want, including the behaviors you desire from others.

Again, this change in mindset will feel subtle, especially in the beginning, but I promise you'll see a payoff if you stick with it.

Here is your growth opportunity: speak in positives instead of negatives, focus on solutions instead of problems, and say what you want instead of what you don't want.

Below are a few examples of these:

Negative Focus
Don't forget our date on Saturday.

Positive Focus
Remember we have a date on Saturday.

Negative Focus
You have to *stop disrespecting* me.

Positive Focus
I'd like you *to treat me with more respect.*

Negative Focus
I *don't* want to be around people like *that.*

Positive Focus
I *want* to be around people like *this.*

Negative Focus
We never spend time together.

Positive Focus
I'd like to spend more time together.

At the end of Section Five:

You have decided to shift your focus from the negative to the positive by making subtle changes in the way you communicate and the language you use. You are telling your partner what you want instead of what you do not want. And you are teaching your brain to focus on the positive aspects of your life and your relationships.

Begin by replacing "Don't Forget" with "Remember" and go from there.

Section Five Tweetable: "I utilize positive language and communication to shift my mindset from what I do not want to what I do want. **@JustinMGMendez**"

Journal

_____

_____

_____

_____

_____

_____

_____

_____

_____

_____

_____

_____

_____

_____

_____

_____

_____

_____

_____

_____

_____

_____

_____

_____

_____

The way we see the world is different at different times and is based around what we are focused on at that point in time.

_____

_____

_____

_____

_____

_____

_____

_____

_____

_____

_____

_____

_____

Speak in positives instead of negatives,
focus on solutions instead of problems,
say what you want instead of what you don't.

_____

_____

_____

_____

_____

_____

_____

_____

_____

Six

Consistency and Perseverance

I would like to leave you with one last section to help develop the benefits of all the others:

As mentioned in Section Two, consistency plays an integral role in building and maintaining trust. This is because being consistent lets others know what they can expect from us in a variety of different situations.

Consistency also determines the direction of our lives and ultimately our future. If you consistently eat junk food every day and exercise once a month what direction is your life headed in? What does your future have in store? Your future will be defined by the activities you repeat on a regular basis, not those that are done here or there.

What is true for life is true for our relationships. If you want your partner to know you care you must consistently give them reasons to do so. If you want to be trusted you must consistently act in a trustworthy manner. And if you want to have clear communication you must consistently practice good communication techniques. I urge you to maintain consistency in the positive things you do.

The beauty of consistency truly lies in its ability to make our outcomes more predictable. This takes much of the guesswork and uncertainty out of life. Baking a cake is a simple example of consistency and predictable outcomes. If you use the same ingredients and follow the same recipe every time you are going to end up with the same cake. But as soon as you stray from the formula, putting two cups of salt instead of sugar, for example, you get a different result. Be consistent with your actions and you will be able to better predict your outcome.

Perseverance is the power to get up after we have fallen down; it is the power to learn from our mistakes and keep moving forward, no matter what the obstacle, until we achieve our goals. It is the nature of all life to persevere, but as human beings we sometimes convince ourselves that we are incapable of sticking it out through tough times and as a result we give up.

If you do not believe that perseverance is in your nature let me remind you that you had to fail repeatedly just to learn the basic activities you now take for granted like the ability to walk, talk, and read. Each of these is the result of a long process of continual effort and of your ability to brush yourself off and keep going, in other words, *to persevere*.

You may be discouraged by your failures. You may break a commitment you made to yourself or to your partner. You are human, you will slip. Keep in mind that your goal is progress, not perfection. The only way to make progress is to continue moving forward.

Just remember, perseverance is in your nature. Whether you believe in Creationism, Evolution, or something else entirely, you are built for success. And again, what is true in life is true in our relationships. Stay consistent and persevere in the face of failure and difficulty.

Do not be fooled by success either. Do not allow your successes to make you lax in practicing the activities which transformed you and your relationships. Let me give an example of what I mean by this.

Imagine you decide to go on a road trip across the United States starting in New York City and working your way to San Francisco. You load up your car with snacks and clothes, fill up your gas tank and begin your journey.

After many hours of driving you realize you need gas. You pull over at the next station, fill up your tank and continue driving.

The trip is going great. Every now and then you realize you need gas so you pull over and fill up. You are making great time and have even had a chance to stop at various historical and scenic destinations along the way.

By the time you reach Colorado your road trip is going so well that you decide to stop worrying about your gas tank, after all, everything is going great so why worry?

We can all imagine how this story ends; it is rather obvious that a car needs gas to continue driving (or an electric car needs a charge).

I use this silly example to make an exaggerated point about the erroneous view many people have of relationships and life in general; which is that if things are going well, our mission is accomplished and whatever benefits we are experiencing will simply continue without any further action from us.

Consistency and perseverance are what keep the gas tank of our relationships full. The benefits of success are merely the world's way of telling us that we should continue on our present course. Stay consistent and persevere.

At the end of Section Six

You understand that in order to transform your relationship you will need both consistency and perseverance.

You are committed to practicing each activity suggested in this book on a consistent basis in the face of both adversity and success.

You realize that perseverance is in your nature and you are dedicated to rise when you fall, learn when you fail, and continue to move forward no matter what.

Section Six Tweetable: #1 "Consistency determines the state of my life & my future. I take positive action consistently to make my outcomes predictable **@JustinMGMendez**"

Section Six Tweetable #2 "It is in my nature to persevere and succeed. When I fall, I rise. When I fail I learn. I grow in my relationships and life. **@JustinMGMendez**"

Journal

_____

_____

_____

_____

_____

_____

_____

_____

_____

_____

_____

_____

_____

*Perseverance is the power to get up
after we've fallen down.
It is the power to learn from our
mistakes and keep moving forward,
no matter what the obstacle...*

Perseverance is in your nature.

_____

_____

_____

_____

_____

_____

_____

_____

_____

_____

_____

The benefits of success are merely the world's way of telling us that we should continue on our present course.

_____

_____

_____

_____

_____

_____

AFTERWARD

As mentioned at the beginning of this book, I have done my best to keep my suggestions simple and actionable; I hope you have found them to be so and I hope you take action.

Sure, you can be like I was two years ago wishing your partner would change so you can finally feel fulfilled in your relationship (in which case you will likely be waiting forever) or you can take responsibility for yourself and start building the relationship you both want and deserve.

Side Note:

While writing this book it occurred to me that some of you may not be in a relationship worth working on. That statement sounds harsh but it is the truth. So all I can say is this:

When you decide to take 100% responsibility for your life, when you realize that you are the solution to your problems and that no one but yourself is responsible for your life or your feelings, please also realize that the solution may very well be to leave the relationship.

Perhaps the only thing worse than being in an abusive relationship and not realizing it is being in an abusive relationship, realizing it, and staying in it. If you are in a verbally, physically, emotionally, or otherwise abusive relationship I suggest walking away.

Take some time to yourself, evaluate what patterns and behaviors attracted that person and that relationship into your life, make some adjustments, and move on to a healthy, supportive, loving relationship.

The great Jim Rohn once said, "If you will change, everything will change for you."

If you want your relationship or your life to improve, you must improve. The state of our lives is a reflection of ourselves; use the steps suggested in this book to create a new image of yourself for your life to reflect. Change the activities you practice every day and you will change the direction of your life.

I have used every suggestion in this book to transform my own relationships and I can promise a healthy, loving, supportive relationship is in your future if you will take my suggestions and make them a part of your life.

In humble and sincere appreciation,
Justin M.G. Mendez
Justin Mendez, LLC

Justin M.G. Mendez

ABOUT THE AUTHOR

Justin M.G. Mendez is America's Youngest Leadership Communication Expert. Justin is an award-winning speaker who offers keynote speeches as well as training presentations, books, ebooks and coaching services.
His expertise covers a wide range of topics from effective communication and leadership to the art of cultivating a truly enjoyable life.

For booking information or to download the audio version of this book, please visit:
www.JustinMGMendez.com

Twitter: **@JustinMGMendez**
Instagram: **@JustinMendez**
YouTube: **youtube.com/user/justinmgmendez**
LinkedIn: **linkedin.com/in/justinmgmendez**

Email: **Justin@JustinMgMendez.com**

Justin M.G. Mendez

SUGGESTED READING

There are many books and many authors I would suggest reading, in fact, there are too many to list.
Here are a few books that are relevant relationships to get you started:

Results Not Typical by Justin M.G. Mendez

The Speed of Trust by Stephen M.R. Covey

A Conscious Person's Guide to Relationships by Ken Keyes, Jr.

The Compound Effect by Darren Hardy

The Four Agreements by Don Miguel Ruiz

The Seasons of Life by Jim Rohn

Made in the USA
San Bernardino, CA
08 October 2014